SECRET IN A
SEALED BOTTLE

SECRET IN A SEALED BOTTLE

Lazzaro Spallanzani's Work with Microbes

by

Sam and Beryl Epstein

Illustrated by

Jane Sterrett

Coward, McCann & Geoghegan, Inc.
New York

Library of Congress Cataloging in Publication Data

Epstein, Sam.   Secret in a sealed bottle.
(Science discovery books)
Bibliography: p.

SUMMARY: A biography of the 18th century Italian whose experiments with microbes disproved the theory of spontaneous generation and provided a base for the work of future scientists.

1. Spallanzani, Lazzaro, 1729–1799—Juvenile literature.   2. Spontaneous generation—Juvenile literature.   3. Biologists—Italy—Biography—Juvenile literature.   [1. Spallanzani, Lazzaro, 1729–1799.   2. Biologists.   3. Spontaneous generation.]   I. Epstein, Beryl Williams. Joint author.   II. Sterrett, Jane.   III. Title.

QH31.S63E67   574'.092'4   [B]   [92]   78-1494
ISBN 0-698-30700-3 lib. bdg.

Printed in the United States of America

CONTENTS

1

What's the Professor Up To?

The sound of shattering glass came through the closed study door. Students in the corridor outside stopped talking and looked at each other.

"I hope the professor isn't hurt," one said.

"He probably just dropped something," another suggested.

"Language dictionaries don't sound like that when they're dropped," the first student pointed out. "Or mathematics textbooks either."

Both of them took the French, Greek and mathematics courses taught by the Abbé Lazzaro Spallanzani. He was their favorite professor of the New College in Reggio Emilia, in the Duchy of Este, one of the small states later united to form the Italian nation.

"But you know how many other things he's interested in," a third student said. Then he grinned. "Perhaps he's been examining a bottle of wine."

They all grinned with him. Everyone knew how much the professor enjoyed good food and good wine.

"I remember now!" the first student said suddenly. "I saw him carry a lot of bottles into his study a few days ago, and they weren't wine bottles. They were a different shape. And they were all empty," he added. "What do you suppose he's up to?"

It was a question none of them could answer.

At that moment, behind the closed study door, Spallanzani was staring down at the remains of the narrow-necked bottle that had contained some of the broth he'd made that morning. It had slipped from the tongs with which he was lifting it to a shelf. Now the steaming broth was a spreading puddle on the room's stone floor.

His big nose wrinkled in disgust as he bent his stocky figure to clean up the mess.

"Perhaps I should give up these experiments before I've squandered my whole salary on glassware," he muttered to himself. This was the third bottle he'd broken in two days, and bottles were expensive. A common wine bottle often would cost more than the wine it held!

But Spallanzani knew he wouldn't abandon the experiments he'd scarcely begun. These experiments offered him the chance he'd been hoping for—the chance to become known as a naturalist.

So, as soon as he'd swept up the splinters of glass and dried the floor, he picked up another bottle and went back to work. Spallanzani hoped to learn how microbes—in his time they were called "little beasties" or animalcules—got into tightly corked bottles of broth, such as he'd been preparing. From the answer to that question, he hoped to learn the answer to still another one—a question that scientists had been arguing heatedly for years. And that question was: Where do the "little beasties" come from?

Today most people know a great deal about microbes, those tiny forms of animal and plant life that can be seen only through a microscope and that are so important to life—and death—on the planet earth.

We now know that untold millions of them exist in the sea, in ponds, in the earth, on rotting vegetable and animal matter, and in hundreds of other places. We also know that they are airborne—that they are carried about by the air.

But microbes were completely unknown until about three hundred years ago, when scientists first had microscopes powerful enough to make them visible. And for the century following their discovery, little was known about them. A few scientists thought that microbes might be airborne, but most people laughed at the idea that these tiny things were floating about in the air. Lazzaro Spallanzani was the first man to *prove* that microbes are airborne. Thus, over two hundred years ago, this Italian scientist took the first important step toward our present understanding of the whole microbial world.

2

Young Man from Scandiano

Lazzaro Spallanzani was born in 1729 and spent his early boyhood in his father's handsome tower-topped house in Scandiano, a small village in the Duchy of Este. At fifteen he was sent to the neighboring town of Reggio Emilia to study at its Catholic seminary. Young Spallanzani proved to be such a brilliant student that he was urged to become a priest in the Dominican order and devote his life to study.

But Spallanzani's father, a prosperous lawyer, expected his son to follow in his own footsteps. So instead of becoming a Dominican, Spallanzani was sent to the great city of Bologna to study law at its famous old university.

Probably Spallanzani would have made a good lawyer—he talked well and loved to argue. But at Bologna University he found himself drawn toward a field that had nothing to do with law. He first learned about this new field through his remarkable cousin, Laura Bassi, who taught experimental physics at the University. And, through her, he became acquainted with Antonio Vallisneri, a professor of the fairly new subject of natural history at the University of Padua, some seventy-five miles south of Bologna.

Even though Spallanzani was studying law, he somehow found time to attend some of his cousin's lectures and some classes in natural history. By letter he developed a friendship with Professor Vallisneri, who himself had come from Scandiano and knew of the Spallanzani family.

Eighteenth-century naturalists—as Vallisneri and his fellow-scientists were called—are recognized today as the pioneers of modern botany, zoology, biology and geology. Their goal was to understand nature and to discover what they called the "laws of nature" that govern it. This goal often set them at odds with the Catholic Church, which emphasized that human beings should simply wonder at the mysteries God had created in His world. The naturalists, and other eighteenth-century scientists too, insisted that since God had given human beings the power to think, He expected them to use that power to unravel those mysteries. And by continuing to question occurrences in nature, those pioneers had already made some important discoveries.

The Englishman Isaac Newton, for example, had studied the mystery of the apparent attraction that the earth has for any object let loose in the air. And he saw that this "attraction" exists not only for objects which fall toward the earth, but also between bodies in space, such as the earth and the moon. He had given the name "gravity" to this power of attraction. And finally, by questioning and experimenting, Newton had discovered the Law of Gravitation: the precise formula for determining the force of gravity between any two bodies in the universe.

Another important discovery had been made in Sweden by a man named Carolus Linnaeus. Linnaeus said that all known plants and animals could be arranged into groups, or families, and that all the members of each group were alike in certain ways. Linnaeus was able to fit into his "system" every one of the strange new plants and animals that were then being brought back to Europe by the explorers of America and other distant places. His system seemed to prove that there was a definite order in all nature.

Discoveries like those made by Newton and Linnaeus were quickly shared with other scientists all over Europe. They were reported in letters sent from one university to another and they were discussed at meetings of scientific societies. Spallanzani heard about these new discoveries in the lectures he was attending.

Of course, as Spallanzani soon learned, many things were still unknown, or not yet understood, or were being argued about. One subject for argument was the creation of animal and plant life. Before anyone had seen a microbe, most naturalists agreed that there was a law of nature which governed the creation of all life. They put the law this way: Every form of life comes from parents of the same kind as itself. These naturalists argued for their belief by pointing out that human beings, animals and insects all come from parents—that even plants come from parent plants.

But in 1675, when the Dutch lens grinder Anton van Leeuwenhoek discovered microbes with his homemade microscopes, some naturalists changed their minds. These naturalists simply couldn't believe— couldn't even imagine—that such tiny forms of life could produce even

tinier "children" that would then "grow up" and produce children themselves. So they said that animalcules must be produced by what they called "spontaneous generation." They meant that animalcules came into being—poof! just like that!—out of the pond water, meat, broth or whatever substance they were found in.

"Nonsense!" said those who believed that all forms of life must be created in the same way. "There is no such thing as spontaneous generation! Even animalcules must be born to parents, or come from parents' eggs or seeds."

And so the argument continued. In Bologna, as elsewhere in Europe, it went on among university students and their professors. It also went on outside the universities, among merchants and noblemen, housewives and servant girls. Somehow this question captured everyone's imagination.

Spallanzani believed that all forms of life, including microbes, must be born of parents. It made nature seem more orderly. And he was glad that his older and more experienced friend, Vallisneri, took the same side of the argument. Vallisneri also believed that animalcules floated about in the air until they settled down on some substance that nourished them, where they then produced their young.

"Of course, no one has actually proved that they have parents," Vallisneri reminded Spallanzani. "But," he added, "neither has anyone proved that they are created by spontaneous generation. The problem of how animalcules come into being is one of the many problems we naturalists hope to solve someday."

Spallanzani had a problem of his own by then. He had decided he wanted to become a naturalist. Seeking and trying to understand the laws of nature seemed to him far more exciting than learning about man-made laws. But he was a dutiful and devoted son. He would become the lawyer his father wanted him to be—unless his father changed his mind.

Vallisneri, and Laura Bassi too, thought Spallanzani had the makings of a really good naturalist, and that his talents would be wasted on law. So Vallisneri went to Scandiano to see if he could change the mind of his friend's father. He returned to Bologna with the news that Spallanzani's father would not stand in the way of his son's choice to become a naturalist.

Spallanzani shut his law books for the last time. He had been set free to begin the studies that would make him one of the greatest scientists of the eighteenth century.

3

The Challenge

When Spallanzani was twenty-five he had finished his studies and was ready to become a professor himself. Of course, he hoped to teach natural history. But in order to earn his living, he took the first post he was offered—professor of French, Greek and mathematics at the New College in Reggio Emilia, the town where he had once been a brilliant seminary student.

There, in spite of his teaching duties, he managed to study theology and become a priest. As the Abbé Spallanzani he had more authority than a mere professor, and a welcome extra income from the Church. Spallanzani never hid the fact that he liked to eat well and live comfortably.

But Spallanzani's greatest interest remained the study of natural history. On his long walks through the rich valley of Este, and in the hills beyond it, he found many things that stirred his naturalist's curiosity.

Once, idly tossing stones at a pond, he remembered how his physics

books explained the fact that stones sometimes skip across the water's surface before sinking. The book said the stones "bounced" off the water because water was "elastic."

"That's ridiculous!" Spallanzani thought suddenly. "If water were elastic, I could fill a water bottle to the top, and then squeeze the water down and make room for more. And that, of course, is impossible."

What, then, was the true explanation of why stones skipped? Finally Spallanzani was able to answer that question by the use of mathematical equations and diagrams. A stone skipped, he wrote in a paper he sent his cousin Laura, because it struck the water a glancing blow, formed a small hollow in the pond's surface, and then "rode up" the slope of the hollow into the air again.

Laura Bassi found the paper very impressive; so did Vallisneri. As a result Vallisneri devised a scheme he hoped would win his young friend recognition as a naturalist.

Many people were saying, just then, that the lively, and sometimes bitter, argument over the existence of spontaneous generation had finally ended. They said it had been settled by the great French naturalist, Count Buffon. In his most recent book Buffon had declared that animalcules were *indeed* created by spontaneous generation, and that this process could now be understood and explained. The series of experiments Buffon's book reported, and which he said proved his theory beyond a doubt, had been carried out by another well-known naturalist, the English priest John Needham.

Vallisneri sent Spallanzani a copy of Buffon's book and a letter.

"I do not need to remind you," Vallisneri wrote, "that Buffon and Father Needham are among our most respected naturalists. And their explanation of the theory of spontaneous generation appears to be reasonable. But I, and other naturalists, still tend to believe that animalcules, like all other living things, have parents. We think it might be useful if someone conducted experiments with these forms of life, to determine once and for all whether or not they come into being by spontaneous generation. I believe you could devise and carry out such experiments, if you will."

Spallanzani was so flattered that he wanted to accept the challenge immediately. What faith Vallisneri had in him!

But then he became cautious. He had never worked in a laboratory and had none to work in now. Would he even know how to begin an experiment?

Nevertheless, the idea of pitting himself against the great Buffon and the English priest was very tempting. If he managed to prove that Buffon was wrong—why, he would become famous in the world of natural history overnight!

Then Spallanzani sternly reminded himself that no good naturalist should set out to prove or disprove anything. He should have only one purpose: to learn the truth.

"Very well!" Spallanzani decided. "I shall seek the truth. My first step must be to read—and to read most carefully—Count Buffon's book."

He read late that night, and during every spare moment of the next several days. He read some passages a dozen times. Finally he had to admit that Buffon's explanation of spontaneous generation did indeed make it sound reasonable.

This, briefly, is what Buffon claimed: In every living thing—whether a plant or an animal—there are many tiny particles, which cannot be destroyed. Buffon called them molecules. When a plant or animal dies, some of those separate particles may come together to form animalcules.

Father Needham agreed with Buffon's theory and had added to it an idea of his own. He said that each of those tiny particles possessed a mysterious "force," and that it was this force that brought them together to form animalcules. Needham called this the Vegetative Force.

Spallanzani had no trouble understanding the experiments Needham had done. For each experiment the English priest had begun with a broth made by boiling water which contained some organic matter— meat, vegetables, grains or grasses. Boiling the broth, Needham said, killed any animalcules that might have been in the water or in the organic material originally.

Spallanzani nodded complete agreement over that statement. Like everyone he knew, he believed that heat destroyed all forms of life.

Needham had then poured his freshly boiled broth into a clean bottle, and corked the bottle so that no one could say animalcules had later entered it from the air outside. After letting the bottle stand for several days, Needham had withdrawn its cork, examined the broth, and found it swarming with animalcules. He had repeated this experiment dozens of times, always with the same result.

Needham had therefore proved—Buffon's book stated—that the animalcules in his broth could have come into existence in only one way: They had been created when the Vegetative Force brought together tiny particles from the meat or other once-living substances in the broth.

Animalcules had been created, in other words, without having had any animalcule parents—by spontaneous generation.

By the time Spallanzani finally put down Buffon's book, he knew he would try to do what Vallisneri wanted him to do. He would begin in the only way he could think of, by repeating Needham's experiments. In that way, at least, he would gain some experience in laboratory work. While he cooked broth, and filled and corked his bottles, and let them stand until it was time to open them again—perhaps, while all that was going on, he might also be able to think up other experiments he could do on his own. Then he might succeed in finding the truth about animalcules "once and for all," as his friend put it.

Spallanzani reached for his quill pen and a sheet of paper, and began his reply to Vallisneri.

4

The First Experiments

The day after those students in the corridor had heard the sound of shattering glass, Spallanzani once more shut himself in his study. He had hurried there as soon as he had dismissed his last class of the day, eager to get to work in the makeshift laboratory he had set up.

His microscope was a good one for the time, though far less powerful than instruments used today. Near it was a charcoal burner, some glass rods, a pair of tongs, a knife, several pots, a funnel and clay jars that held various kinds of seeds and grains. A shelf above his microscope table had been cleared for his round-bellied, long-necked bottles— empty ones on the right, those already containing broth on the left.

He began by putting water into a pot and adding to it small pieces of the mutton he had bought at the market that morning. Then he set the pot over the charcoal burner and fanned the gray coals to a red glow. While the broth heated he washed two of his unused bottles, the second bottle as a kind of insurance in case the first one broke. From a box of corks he chose the two that fitted the bottles best.

Suddenly his mutton broth was bubbling. He dribbled a little of it into each of his bottles and swirled it around. Only when he was sure the glass had been warmed did he pour in enough additional broth to make the bottle about a third full. Then he corked them snugly, labeled them with the date and the kind of broth they contained, and added them to the row of filled bottles already on his shelf.

Now came the moment he'd been looking forward to. The first corked bottles he had placed on the shelf had been there for three days—the length of time Needham had let his bottles stand before examining their contents.

Spallanzani cleared a space around his microscope, lifted down one bottle, and uncorked it. The broth in it had been made from barley. Three days ago it had had the good clean smell of grain. Now it smelled "spoiled" and Spallanzani's big nose twitched in disgust.

He reached for a glass rod and lowered it into the bottle. Slowly he drew it out. A drop of broth clung to its tip. He let the drop fall onto a slide—a small rectangle of thin glass—and set the slide in place beneath his microscope.

He forgot the unpleasant smell of the broth as he bent down to look through the eyepiece of his microscope.

At first he saw only a blur. Patiently he adjusted the lens.

There they were! He was seeing just what Needham claimed he had seen under his own microscope: a swarm of wriggling animalcules. Some were round, others were oval and fringed around the edge. A third group appeared to be rod-shaped. Spallanzani stared intently at all of them for a long time.

"Yes," he muttered finally. "Animalcules have indeed appeared in this broth, just as the book said they would."

He straightened up and stared into space.

"Now the only remaining question is whether or not they were created by spontaneous generation. And that question," he added, his voice rising, "is, in my opinion, not settled by this experiment!"

"I beg your pardon, Professor!" a voice said.

Spallanzani turned toward the door and glimpsed the back of a swiftly departing student. "Come back, Carlo!" he called.

"I'm sorry to interrupt you when you have a guest," Carlo apologized as he entered the room.

"A guest?" Spallanzani was puzzled. Then he realized he had been speaking aloud. "No, no, Carlo," he said, smiling. "My only guest is in my mind. I am arguing with an Englishman, a Father Needham. Come, I'll show you what we are arguing about."

Carlo moved eagerly across the room. Yesterday, in the corridor with his friends, he had wondered what his professor was up to. Now his curiosity was going to be satisfied!

"Look through this microscope, Carlo," the Abbé Spallanzani was saying. "What do you see?"

"Are those what are called animalcules, Professor?"

"They are," Spallanzani nodded. "Now I'll ask you a question. Is there such a thing as spontaneous generation?"

"I don't know," Carlo admitted. "Many of my friends argue about it, but I don't know enough to make up my mind."

"Excellent!" Spallanzani said. "Always learn the facts before making a decision." Then he told Carlo about Buffon's book and the Needham experiments which he himself was now repeating.

"So the animalcules you have seen are in the broth from one of my corked bottles which has been on the shelf for three days," he concluded. "According to Father Needham, they were created out of that broth by spontaneous generation."

"Do you believe that, Professor?" Carlo asked.

"Let us say I doubt it," Spallanzani answered carefully. "You see, Father Needham claims his corks fitted so well that it was as if his bottles were 'hermetically sealed.' My corks also fitted very well. But to seal anything hermetically is to make it completely, perfectly airtight!"

"I see!" Carlo said. "And you think a cork does not seal hermetically—that air can get past it, as wine sometimes leaks past a wine bottle's cork. And you think animalcules—or their eggs or seeds—could get into the bottle with the air!"

"I say only that a cork *may* let air in," Spallanzani corrected him. "But for that reason I feel Father Needham's method has left some doubts about his claims. Surely a good naturalist," he went on, beginning to pace the room, "could devise a better experiment—one whose results could not be doubted."

Carlo waited for him to speak again. But soon he realized the professor was no longer aware of him, and Carlo slipped out of the room. He'd forgotten the question about his Greek lesson that he'd come to ask. He was in a hurry to tell his friends what the Abbé Spallanzani was doing with all those bottles.

26

5

Sealed Bottles

After examining the broth in that first bottle, Spallanzani felt fairly certain that he would find animalcules in the broth of every one of the other bottles he had prepared by Needham's method. The days that followed proved him right.

But he went on, stubbornly experimenting with all the different kinds of broth Needham had used. It took him many weeks. The hours he spent in his laboratory had to be squeezed out of his busy schedule of study and teaching.

For a time his bottles still cracked or burst fairly often. He burned his hands and stained his clothes. But gradually he became so deft and sure that such accidents almost never occurred. He was continually teaching himself new laboratory skills.

When he had completed all the experiments Needham had made, Spallanzani was more than ready to tackle the new experiments he'd been planning. He wanted to put broth into bottles that were truly hermetically sealed, and he thought he had figured out a way to do this.

Then suddenly he was offered the kind of job he'd long hoped for. He was invited to teach natural history at the University of Modena, capital of the Duchy of Este and its most important city.

Abbé Spallanzani knew he would enjoy living near the great Ducal Palace and he was pleased that Modena was only a short distance from Scandiano. He would still be close to his family. He wanted particularly to keep his eye on his young sister Marianna, who showed promise of becoming a good naturalist herself. But the most important thing, of course, was that he would be able to give all his time to the world of natural history. And he would have a real laboratory, a larger and more convenient place than the crowded corner of his study.

Spallanzani moved to Modena and settled into new quarters. There were new class schedules to be worked out and new students to meet. All this took time. But finally he was ready to start his new experiments.

He began as he had so often before, by making a pot of broth and preparing some clean bottles. But this time, after pouring some broth into his first bottle, he didn't seal it with a cork. Using his tongs to pick the bottle up by its long neck, he held it on the far side of his charcoal fire. Next, he put the thin tube of a blowpipe into his mouth and blew through it to force a stream of air into the fire. The air drove a blue tongue of flame straight at the top of the bottle's neck. Spallanzani turned the bottle slowly to heat the glass all around.

The top of the neck became red hot and began to soften. When the glass was about to melt, Spallanzani pinched the neck with another pair of tongs. The glass flowed together, under the tongs, as smoothly as liquid. There was no longer an opening into the bottle. It had been completely sealed off.

28

Spallanzani set the bottle down gently and took the blowpipe out of his mouth. The glass was already hardening again. The process he had just completed was very different from simply pushing a cork into the bottle's neck.

"This bottle," he said to himself with satisfaction, as he labeled it and put in on the shelf, "is now truly hermetically sealed. Nothing—not even the slightest breath of air—can get into it!"

During the rest of that day, and the next two days, that bottle was joined by several dozen others. But on the fourth day Spallanzani didn't bother to light his charcoal fire. This was the day on which he would examine the contents of the first bottles he had sealed. The next few moments could decide his future. If there were no animalcules in the broth, he could say he had proved that Father Needham and the great Count Buffon were wrong.

"But suppose the animalcules are there!" he muttered.

Their presence, of course, would mean he had actually proved Buffon's theory—and proved it even more dramatically than Needham had done! Since he was sure no air could have entered his sealed bottle, he would not be able to suggest that the animalcules had come from air entering the bottle past its cork. And in that case the only logical explanation for their presence would be spontaneous generation.

Spallanzani knew how hard it would be for him to accept the presence of animalcules, and how difficult it would be to report their presence to Vallisneri. Still, he wouldn't be able to deny the result of his own work, unless he were willing to admit that he had made some serious mistake in his experiment. And he didn't think he had made any mistake.

30

"But if there are no animalcules—" Spallanzani cut off the words. There would be time enough to enjoy that triumph if his eyes gave him proof of it.

Carefully he cleaned the lens of his microscope. He set out his slides and a glass rod. He lifted down one of the bottles he had sealed three days before.

Using a small file, he scratched the bottle's neck to weaken it just below where it was sealed. He tapped it lightly at that point, and the sealed top broke off in his hand. He quickly thrust his glass rod into the broth, brought up a drop of the liquid and let it fall on a glass slide. Placing the slide under his microscope, he bent over to focus the lens.

For several long seconds he peered through the eyepiece. He rubbed his eye and looked again.

There was no doubt about what he was seeing. The drop of broth from his carefully sealed bottle was swarming with wriggling animalcules!

6

"Surely It Is Impossible!"

Spallanzani stared down at his microscope. Was it actually true then? Was Buffon's theory correct after all?

Then Spallanzani's head came up with a jerk. He had just realized that spontaneous generation didn't have to be the only explanation for the animalcules he had just seen. There might be another one.

"Perhaps this bottle wasn't perfectly sealed!" he said aloud. He reminded himself that he had never worked with molten glass before. When he thought he was pinching the bottle's neck closed, he might very well have left a tiny opening in it.

He reached for a second bottle and examined its top. There was certainly no flaw in the seal of this one.

Within seconds he had snapped its top off, put a drop of its broth on a slide, and placed the slide under his microscope. He held his breath as he bent over it.

Then he let out his breath in a long, heavy sigh. This batch of broth was also alive with animalcules!

Spallanzani snatched down from the shelf every bottle he had prepared three days before. One after another he examined the broth each bottle contained. In the broth from every bottle he found a lively population of those small wriggling things.

There was nothing more to do after that. He sank into his chair, too tired even for the steady pacing that always helped him to think. But he went on thinking all the same.

He was still sure that he and Vallisneri had good reason to doubt the existence of spontaneous generation. To both of them spontaneous generation seemed to deny the orderliness they believed existed in nature.

If all other living things had parents, wasn't it logical to think that animalcules had parents too? Of course it was!

But the presence of animalcules in the broth from his hermetically sealed bottles was a fact. And, as he had so often told his students, a naturalist's conclusions should be based on facts alone.

Therefore, if no air had gotten into his sealed bottles, and if all the animalcules in them had been killed before the bottles were sealed, then the animalcules he had seen. . . .

Spallanzani sat up suddenly. Was he sure, he asked himself, that all the animalcules in each bottle had been killed before the glass had been sealed?

No, he decided, he couldn't be sure. Even if boiling the broth had killed all the animalcules in that liquid, what about the air he had sealed inside the bottles along with the broth? What about the animalcules in that air?

He knew immediately that he must undertake another series of experiments. This time he would make sure that the air as well as the broth in each sealed bottle was completely free of live animalcules.

The weeks that followed were too crowded with teaching duties to leave him any time for the new experiments he was eager to begin. But finally he was able to return to his laboratory to boil up a batch of broth, pour the broth into clean bottles, and seal the bottles with the flame from his blowpipe. Then Spallanzani put several inches of water in a large vat and set the vat on the fire.

When the water in the vat was boiling, he carefully lowered his bottles into it. He watched them jiggle about in the boiling liquid. Soon the broth inside the bottles was simmering. It was as hot as the boiling water in the vat. This meant that the air in the bottles must also be reaching a satisfactorily high temperature.

Spallanzani congratulated himself on the success of his new method and sat down to add an account of it to the notes he kept on all his experiments.

The notes took longer than he expected. Suddenly he realized that the bottles had been in the vat for a quarter of an hour. He removed them quickly and set them to cool.

But he wasn't sorry he'd left them there for that long. He could be sure now that all life in those particular bottles had been completely destroyed.

Four days later he hurried to the laboratory to examine them. He was smiling confidently as he bent over the microscope.

"Impossible!" he muttered a moment later, and he was no longer smiling. "Surely it is impossible!"

But once again he was staring down at a lively population of animalcules! And there were similar populations in the next two bottles he brought down from the shelf to examine.

He told himself he must look at all those he had prepared by his new method. But suddenly, with several bottles still left to be examined, he had had enough. Leaving his equipment to be cleaned up another day, he slammed shut the door of his laboratory and walked out, heading for the town.

He had accepted Vallisneri's challenge in high spirits. He hadn't minded the long hours of work, stretching over many months, which he had given to his experiments. But he told himself now that it was just as well they were over. He would write a report for Vallisneri of what he had done, and then he would devote himself completely to teaching his students. That was, after all, what a professor was hired to do.

And Buffon's theory would be left as secure as it had been when his book was greeted with such acclaim. Spontaneous generation apparently did exist, however illogical it still seemed to a brash young naturalist from the village of Scandiano.

"Unless I made some mistake, of course," Spallanzani muttered as he strode along crowded sidewalks, through streets noisy with the clop of hooves and the squeaking of wooden wheels.

But he couldn't think *what* that mistake might have been. In fact, he thought he could take considerable pride in the care and skill with which he had carried out his experiments. He could be sure of just two things at the moment, he told himself. The first was that he had learned a good deal about laboratory work. The second was that there had been

as many animalcules in the broth of his hermetically sealed and boiled bottles as there had ever been in the broth of his corked bottles prepared by Needham's method.

Then he stopped short in the middle of the sidewalk. A woman with a heavy market basket glared when she had to walk around him. Spallanzani didn't notice.

"But am I really sure that there were an equal number of animalcules in the two different experiments?" he asked aloud.

He started back toward his laboratory. He'd left several bottles unexamined, hadn't he? he asked himself. Yes, he was sure he had.

A group of students talking on a corner moved out of his way when they saw how swiftly he was striding toward them. They didn't attempt to speak to him. They realized he didn't even see them.

Yes, the bottles were there, all right. Spallanzani lost no time opening one of them and examining the drop of broth he took from it.

He couldn't count the tiny living things moving about under his eye. But he had a feeling that this drop was not as crowded as those he had studied on previous days. A feeling wasn't a fact, of course. Still— suppose he was right? What would that mean?

He paced the floor of his laboratory, back and forth, back and forth.

If there had not been quite so many animalcules in the drops from one of these last bottles, did that mean that some had been destroyed during the fifteen minutes in the vat of boiling water? If so, was it possible that the destroyed animalcules were those that had been weakest, and that only the stronger ones were still alive? Would longer boiling destroy the stronger ones too?

Without realizing it, Spallanzani had already begun to clear off his work bench. He would be ready at the earliest possible moment to start a fresh series of experiments that might answer these questions.

There was nothing new about the way he began his work on the next day he was free to spend in his laboratory. He boiled broth, sealed it in bottles, heated a vat of water, and placed the bottles in it.

Then he made a note of the time, and kept a watchful eye on the slowly ticking pendulum clock on his wall.

At the end of half an hour he removed a third of the bottles, labeled them as soon as they were cool, and set them on a shelf.

At the end of a full hour another third of the bottles came out, to be labeled in their turn.

The final group of bottles stayed in the bubbling vat for an hour and a half before he took them out.

Three days later—days which seemed endlessly long to him—he had his microscope ready for the task of examining the broth in all three groups.

First he placed under his lens a drop of broth from a bottle that had been boiled for half an hour.

Yes! he thought excitedly. He was certain this time. There were half a dozen animalcules clumped together on the right and there were a dozen or so toward the center. But he was sure he had never before found himself looking at such a small population of animalcules.

Spallanzani wasn't interested in exactly how many there were. Swiftly, but with his usual precise care, he prepared another slide with broth from a bottle that had remained in the vat for an hour.

He bent over the microscope. His body stiffened, but he didn't move. Once he blinked his eyes, but he went on staring.

He was staring at a drop of broth that was empty of movement, empty of shapes. In this drop of broth there was not a single animalcule to be seen!

Every one of the bottles that had been boiled for an hour proved free of life. So did all the bottles that had been boiled even longer.

Long boiling had destroyed whatever life had been in the bottles after they had been sealed. And no new life had been created in the broth since that boiling.

Spallanzani wanted to shout his news to the world. He had proved it—he, Lazzaro Spallanzani! There *was* no such thing as spontaneous generation!

7

Another Challenge

Before Spallanzani could write the exciting news to Vallisneri, he thought of something else he wanted to do.

He lined up on a shelf all the bottles in which he had found no animalcules—the bottles that had been in the boiling water for an hour or more. He didn't touch the broken bottle necks. The broth remained open to the air. After several days he examined it all again.

Every drop he peered at through his microscope was now crowded with animalcules.

In his report to Vallisneri, therefore, Spallanzani made two important claims.

He wrote Vallisneri that he had proved animalcules were not created by spontaneous generation—spontaneous generation did not exist. His proof for this was that no animalcules had been created in any sealed bottle that had been boiled long enough to destroy any life it originally contained.

He had also proved, he wrote, that animalcules came from the air.

His proof of this was that they did appear, even in broth that had been free of them, as soon as air was allowed to reach that broth.

Vallisneri was greatly impressed by the report. In 1765—four years after Spallanzani had first read Buffon's book—the report was published so that other naturalists could read it too. The result was that Spallanzani, now thirty-six years old, quickly gained recognition as one of the leading naturalists of Europe.

Neither Count Buffon nor Father Needham applauded him, but dozens of other naturalists did. They called Spallanzani's proofs completely convincing. They also praised him for devising brilliant experiments, and for carrying them out with remarkable skill and precision. They honored him by making him a member of some of the most important scientific societies of the time—the Royal Society of England, and the similar societies of Prussia, Sweden, Germany, Switzerland and several Italian cities.

Spallanzani felt he deserved all the honors he received, for having settled "once and for all" the question of spontaneous generation. But he was especially pleased by his invitation to join the society in Bologna. Bologna was where he had first been introduced to the world of nature.

As it turned out, though, the question of spontaneous generation still wasn't settled in everyone's mind. Many people who had always believed in it continued to cling to their belief. Nevertheless, since the naturalists Spallanzani most respected were convinced by his proofs, he felt free to turn his attention to other still unanswered questions. He had always been "burning with curiosity," as he once wrote about himself. Now he was curious about a dozen things.

He became busier than he'd ever been before. He taught, he corresponded with other naturalists all over Europe (and sometimes journeyed to visit them), and he performed experiments that added further to his reputation among his admirers.

For a time his shelves were crowded with boxes of earthworms and snails, cages of toads and salamanders, and tanks of tadpoles and water worms. He operated on hundreds of these creatures, cutting off parts of their bodies to learn whether they could grow new parts to replace them. By cutting off the heads of seven hundred snails he discovered that a headless snail could usually grow a new head. He also learned that when a water worm was cut into several pieces, each piece became a whole new worm.

From his experiments with salamanders he became the first man to learn how blood can travel through even the tiniest, most twisted blood vessel. Using equipment he had to invent for himself, he discovered that the corpuscles in the blood could, as he wrote, "change shape and pass through the sharpest bends and folds."

Spallanzani's increasing fame brought him an offer to teach at the University of Pavia and to take charge of its natural history museum. Pavia had not long before fallen into the hands of Austria, whose triumphant armies had been enlarging the Austrian Empire. The offer, therefore, came from Austria's queen, Maria Theresa. She was determined to make Pavia an important center of learning.

There were ancient and magnificent palaces in Pavia, and a majestic cathedral. But the University, and especially the University's natural history museum, had been neglected for years. Maria Theresa was willing to pay the well-known Spallanzani a great deal of money to improve the museum and lend the glory of his own name to the University.

Spallanzani enjoyed all the traveling he had been doing the last few years. He had discovered that a journey, like an experiment, was an opportunity to learn and explore. But he had never lived outside the borders of his native Duchy of Este, and would have been content to make his home within the Duchy for the rest of his life, close to his own village of Scandiano.

However, he couldn't resist the splendid salary he'd been offered by Maria Theresa and he found the idea of directing Pavia's natural history museum especially appealing. He could imagine himself seeking new specimens for the museum in strange corners of the world, all at the expense of the Austrian queen. In addition, he thought his young sister Marianna would enjoy helping him arrange the museum's displays. So he accepted the queen's offer and told Marianna she would go with him to his new post.

Shortly before leaving for Pavia, Spallanzani learned that his report on spontaneous generation had been translated into French. He was pleased to think that now Frenchmen could read in their own language his clear proof that their famous Count Buffon had been wrong.

Soon after this news he received a copy of the French translation, and found that something had been added to his report. Printed along with it was a strong attack on his work. The attack came from Father Needham.

Needham declared that Spallanzani had by no means proved that spontaneous generation did not exist. Instead, Needham said, Spallanzani's method of sealing and boiling the bottles had made it impossible for spontaneous generation to take place.

An hour or more of boiling, Needham went on to say, would always seriously damage the fragile Vegetative Force—the force he claimed brought particles of dead organic material together to form animalcules. When that force was damaged, Needham declared, spontaneous generation couldn't take place. And that, he said, was why there had been no animalcules in Spallanzani's well-boiled bottles.

"Nonsense!" Spallanzani said angrily.

Then he read on. Father Needham also claimed that the air in Spallanzani's bottles had been damaged, and that the Vegetative Force could not operate in damaged air.

To prove that the air had been damaged, Needham said, he had repeated Spallanzani's experiments. He had sealed, boiled, cooled and opened bottles of broth. But when he opened the bottles, he had heard air rushing into them. Air would not have rushed into the bottles, Needham said, unless the air inside them had lost some of its "elasticity."

Spallanzani knew what Needham meant when he wrote about the air's elasticity. The word was then generally used to express the fact that air can be squeezed, or compressed, and that it can also be expanded or thinned out. Spallanzani had to admit he hadn't noticed air rushing in when he opened his sealed bottles, but he realized that it must have occurred. While he heated the neck of a bottle in order to seal it, the air inside the bottle must have become heated too. Since heated air expands, some of the air in the bottle must have been pushed out before the seal was finished. Then, as the bottle cooled, the air inside it would have contracted again, leaving room for more air to rush into the bottle as soon as it was opened. But Spallanzani was very sure that air never lost its elasticity. He was sure it could expand and contract over and over again without being "damaged."

"Father Needham is wrong!" Spallanzani declared. "He is confused. He is befuddled. He is wrong!"

In his first public speech as the new professor of natural history at Pavia, in 1769, Spallanzani made an announcement. He let it be known, in no uncertain terms, that he would settle accounts with Father Needham just as soon as he had the time to do so!

8

Spallanzani Supplies More Proof

One reason Spallanzani was determined to settle his account with the English priest was, of course, his own pride. If he ignored Needham's attack he would appear to be admitting that Needham was right. And that would hurt the reputation he had won as an outstanding naturalist. It would cast doubt on all the various experiments he had done, and even on those he hoped to do in the future.

But the most important reason to answer Needham's attack was that Spallanzani firmly believed his experiments had shown that even the tiniest living things came from parents. And if he were right about that, he had supplied important evidence about the laws governing the world of nature. If more work were necessary to get that evidence established beyond any doubt, Spallanzani was ready to do it.

It wasn't easy to find the time he would need to take up Needham's challenge. Spallanzani now had more students than ever before. And he was doing his best, with Marianna's help, to make Pavia's natural history museum one of the finest in Europe. Months went by before he could settle down in his new laboratory to carry out the task he had set himself.

He put some broth into clean bottles, but this time he left them unsealed and open. Then he poured water into a big vat, placed his bottles in it, and put the vat on the fire. He left the bottles in the boiling water for several hours before removing them and storing them away, still unsealed and open.

Several days later, when he was ready to examine them, some of his students gathered around to watch.

"According to Father Needham," Spallanzani told them, "there will be no animalcules in this broth because its Vegetative Force has been destroyed by long boiling. Let us see."

He bent over the microscope and then let the students peer through the lens. Carefully they examined each sample of broth. Each one—just as Spallanzani had expected—was crowded with tiny forms of life.

"Why are these animalcules present?" Spallanzani demanded, and then proceeded to answer his own question triumphantly. "Because the broth in these bottles has been open to the air!"

For his next experiment he selected several of the different kinds of grain he had often used for making broth. He roasted half of them in a coffee roaster until they were black. The rest he burned in the searing flame of his blowpipe until they were reduced to cinders.

By then his students were ready with their own comments.

"Father Needham would say the Vegetative Force in the particles of those grains has certainly been destroyed by now," one spoke up. "Therefore, he would say, none of the particles of those grains will be able to come together in the form of animalcules."

Spallanzani nodded approvingly at the students as he poured pure boiled water over the grains to make several batches of broth. Again he left the bottles unsealed. Again, after several days, each bottle had its thriving animalcule population.

"And that," Spallanzani said, "should convince even Father Needham that there is no such thing as Vegetative Force—that it has existed only in his imagination."

"You have proved that so clearly that you can now ignore his second complaint, Professor," one student pointed out. "If the Vegetative Force does not exist, it cannot be harmed by damaged air."

Once more Spallanzani nodded approvingly. Then he added, "But until I have completely disposed of his damaged-air theory, there may be those who will doubt the truth of my conclusions."

Before performing his next experiment, he explained to the students why air might rush into a sealed bottle when it was opened.

"That rush of air is what Needham claims as proof of damage," he went on. "And since it occurs when the air in a bottle has been heated just before a bottle is sealed, I must now seal a bottle without permitting the air in it to grow hot."

He began as he usually did when he sealed a bottle of broth. He heated its neck until it grew red hot and softened. The air in the bottle was now expanding, he pointed out to the students, and some of it was being forced out.

He then held the neck of the bottle gently in his tongs, and began to stretch it out. Longer and longer it grew, and thinner and thinner until it was no larger around than a straw. But there was still a tiny opening running through its entire length.

50

While Spallanzani let the bottle cool, he reminded the students that the cooling air in it was now contracting, and that more air was flowing into the bottle through the tiny opening he had left in the long neck. When the bottle was completely cool, he said, it would contain as much air as it had before he had heated it.

As soon as the bottle had cooled to room temperature, Spallanzani moved swiftly. He applied the thin flame of his blowpipe to the upper tip of the bottle's long straw-thin neck. That narrow tube grew red hot almost instantly. In another instant Spallanzani had pinched the soft glass and sealed that tiny opening.

He had worked with such speed that only the very end of the thin neck had been heated. The bottle itself, and the air it contained, had not had time to grow warm. Therefore none of the air had been pushed out of the bottle before its neck had been sealed.

Spallanzani sealed several bottles in the same way, put them all into boiling water for an hour, and then let them stand for three days.

When he was ready to examine them, he lit a candle and held its flame close to the first bottle he would open. If any air rushed into the bottle when it was opened, the motion of the air would make the candle flame waver.

With the skill of long practice, Spallanzani cracked off the bottle's thin neck. No one in the room was breathing.

The candle flame held steady.

"So!" Spallanzani said triumphantly, already tipping the bottle to pour a drop out of its thin neck. "There was no rush of air into the bottle, and therefore even Father Needham could not claim that the elasticity of the bottle's original air has been damaged. Therefore he would have to admit, if he were here, that his Vegetative Force has not been harmed by damaged air. So we should expect to find animalcules in this broth, should we not!"

The students were grinning.

Spallanzani was smiling too, as he straightened up after examining the drop of broth under his lens. "What can have happened?" he asked his audience in mock surprise. "I see no animalcules at all!"

The students too peered at the drop of broth, one after the other. It was, they assured him, empty of any kind of life. So were the samples of broth from all the other bottles Spallanzani opened and examined.

"Now let us leave these bottles open to the air for a few days, and examine the broth again," Spallanzani said, when the day's work was concluded.

And when the broth was examined again, at the end of that time, every sample of it was swarming with animalcules.

"Vegetative Force! Spontaneous generation!" Spallanzani snorted. "They simply do not exist! Air will deposit animalcules on any substance it can reach, along with eggs or seeds from which we must assume animalcules are created. And if the substance is a nourishing one for those creatures, whole populations of them will soon be thriving on it. This is true in my laboratory. It is true in Father Needham's laboratory. It is true everywhere in the world."

9

Born in Scandiano, Known Throughout the World

Charles Bonnet, a famous Swiss naturalist of the time, wrote that his friend Lazzaro Spallanzani had "discovered more truths in five years than entire academies in half a century." Other important scientists agreed with that judgment.

Spallanzani would learn that for years to come some people would still cling to a belief in spontaneous generation. But he knew that his experiments, in response to Needham's attack, had convinced most scientists of the truth about spontaneous generation. Spallanzani felt free to go on to a study of the many other subjects that fascinated him—volcanic gases and rock, eels and other forms of marine life, the process of digestion.

He remained very interested in microbes, however, and he came to know more about them than any other man of his day. Some of the things he learned had to do with how they reproduce themselves. He discovered that the fine bits of "dust" which blow off of molds are actually the "seeds" of these microscopic plants. If they settle on cheese, meat, or other suitable moist organic substances, they grow into new mold families or colonies.

One day Spallanzani read a report by Horace de Saussure, nephew of his good friend Bonnet. Saussure had written that through his microscope he had watched certain rod-shaped animalcules break at the middle into two shorter rods, and then had seen those "pieces" grow larger and divide again!

"This is how these animalcules multiply," Saussure had concluded. "They simply divide—one becomes two."

Spallanzani was delighted to know of this additional way in which microbes come into being. He was angry when an English scientist soon afterward declared Saussure was mistaken. Animalcules might break in two "from bumping into each other," the Englishman said, but he insisted that "the two parts do not become other animalcules."

Spallanzani immediately set out to find a way to establish the truth. And, as usual, he devised a simple but brilliant experiment.

On a microscope slide he put one drop of a broth that was swarming with animalcules. Close to it, but not touching it, he put a drop of pure boiled water containing no life at all. Then he ran the point of a needle from the drop of broth to the drop of water. As the point moved, a thin thread of broth followed it, forming a tiny canal connecting the two drops.

With a small brush in one hand, Spallanzani focused his lens on that canal. Suddenly, one rod-shaped animalcule wriggled into it and then on into the drop of pure water. Before others could follow, Spallanzani destroyed the canal by drawing his brush across it. Now he was ready to settle down and watch that single creature moving about like a lone swimmer in a pool.

For a time nothing happened. Then he realized that the rod-shaped creature was growing thinner and thinner at its middle. In another moment the rod had separated into two parts—and each part swam off by itself!

"It certainly didn't break in two because another animalcule bumped into it!" Spallanzani said.

He went on watching. Half an hour after that first division, each new animalcule divided again, so that there were four. And some thirty minutes after that, the four divided and became eight.

"Saussure is most certainly right!" Spallanzani said. "At least this one kind of animalcule does indeed multiply by dividing!"

Many years later it would be proved that a large variety of microbes reproduce by dividing in the middle, that others split in two lengthwise, and that still others grow buds which break off and become new microbes.

Spallanzani was nearly seventy when an illness forced him to give up some of his many activities. The doctors could do nothing for him. Spallanzani knew the trouble was in his bladder. What he couldn't know then was that it had been caused by some of the microbes he had studied so enthusiastically. But Spallanzani did think that an examination of his bladder, after his death, might lead to some useful knowledge. So he left orders that it was to be removed from his body and turned over to doctors to study.

Spallanzani died on February 11, 1799, shortly after his seventieth birthday. A bronze bust of him now stands on a marble mantel in the house where he was born. The plaque beneath reads:

Born in Scandiano, Known Throughout the World.

EPILOGUE

For many years before his death Spallanzani was widely regarded as the greatest living student of nature. He accepted this tribute as his just due, but it pleased him all the same. He would have been even more pleased if he could have known about the work that other scientists would do in the future, work based on his own discoveries and some of the laboratory techniques he had so skillfully developed.

For example, Spallanzani had performed experiments to learn how food is digested. He had concluded that digestion depended upon a liquid in the stomach—a liquid he named gastric juice. In 1833, Dr. William Beaumont, an American army surgeon who made further experiments with gastric juice, learned much of what is known today about the process of digestion.

Other men based their work on Spallanzani's knowledge of how microbes come into being, and how they can be destroyed. One was Nicholas Appert, a Frenchman. He knew that the boiled broth in Spallanzani's hermetically sealed bottles had remained free of microbes, and thus "unspoiled," for as long as the bottles remained sealed. So, in 1806, Appert boiled several kinds of food and put them in hermetically sealed containers. The food did not spoil so long as the containers remained sealed. Appert, using the process now called sterilization, had invented the method of canning food.

Another nineteenth-century Frenchman who carried on Spallanzani's work with microbes was the great Louis Pasteur. With better equipment than Spallanzani ever dreamed of, Pasteur did some of the same kind of experiments the Italian had done a century earlier. Pasteur, with his flair for showmanship, finally convinced the whole world that Spallanzani had indeed been right—that microbes were never spontaneously generated. Pasteur then went on to prove that microbes can cause diseases of plants, animals, and humans. He and other scientists could thus start the long search, still going on today, for ways to prevent and cure the diseases caused by germs.

Pasteur was such a great admirer of Spallanzani that he had the Italian's portrait painted and hung it in his dining room. Then, every day, he could look up and acknowledge his own debt, and the world's, to that stubborn and brilliant experimenter, Lazzaro Spallanzani.

GLOSSARY

ANIMALCULES   The name once used for the tiny forms of life now known as microbes.

CORPUSCLES   Very small cells which float freely in the blood.

GASTRIC JUICE   A fluid in the stomach, necessary for the process of food digestion.

HERMETICALLY SEALED   Closed so perfectly that no air or other gas can enter or escape.

LAW OF NATURE   Any rule or principle of the natural world that always works in the same way under the same conditions, as the Law of Gravitation.

MICROBE (from the Greek word *mikros,* meaning small)   A plant or animal organism so small that it can be seen only through a microscope.

MICROSCOPE   An instrument with a lens, or lenses, which magnifies objects and makes it possible to see things too small to be seen with the naked eye. Believed to have been invented by Hans and Zacharias Janssen, Dutch spectacle-makers, about 1590.

NATURAL HISTORY   The term once used to describe the study of nature—plants, animals and minerals. Today the study of nature is broken down into such sciences as botany, zoology, biology and geology.

NATURALIST   A student of natural history.

ORGANIC MATTER   A substance derived from living organisms, either plant or animal.

SPONTANEOUS GENERATION   The generation or birth of living things from nonliving matter.

VEGETATIVE FORCE   The name once given to a force believed to exist in particles of organic matter, and which brought them together to form microbes by spontaneous generation.

SOME PEOPLE TO KNOW ABOUT

NICHOLAS APPERT (1750–1841) Inventor of a method for preserving food by heating it and sealing it from the air. For this invention, today called canning, he received a 12,000-franc prize from the French government.

LAURA MARIA CATERINA BASSI (1711–1778) Professor of experimental physics at the University of Bologna at a time when few women were scientists. This brilliant woman married and raised a family, but continued to lecture at the University until her death.

WILLIAM BEAUMONT (1785–1853) United States army surgeon who unraveled some of the mysteries of digestion by experimenting on a patient who had a never-healing hole in his stomach.

CHARLES BONNET (1720–1793) Swiss naturalist who studied insects, plants and animals, and who discovered how caterpillars and butterflies breathe and reproduce themselves.

COUNT BUFFON (1707–1788) French naturalist, director of the king's botanical garden and author of a 44-volume *Natural History*.

ANTON VAN LEEUWENHOEK (1632–1723) Dutch shopkeeper and amateur lens grinder who in 1675 looked at a drop of water through his homemade lens and became the first person to see a microbe.

CAROLUS LINNAEUS (1707–1778) Swedish naturalist who arranged all the living things he knew of into groups, in such a way that all members of each group had similar characteristics. He thus laid some of the chief foundations of modern botany and zoology.

JOHN TUBERVILLE NEEDHAM (1713–1781) English priest and naturalist who attempted to prove the theory of spontaneous generation. In his later years he was director of the Brussels Academy of Science.

SIR ISAAC NEWTON (1642–1727) English mathematician and physicist whose many scientific achievements include the discovery of the Law of Gravitation, the theory of color and the mathematical system known as calculus.

LOUIS PASTEUR (1822–1895) French chemist who discovered that microbes can cause diseases of plants and animals, and thus revolutionized the treatment of disease. The process he invented for the preservation of milk and wine is known as pasteurization.

HORACE BENEDICT DE SAUSSURE (1740–1799) Swiss naturalist and mountain climber who spent years studying the geology, meteorology and botany of the Alps. He was probably the first man to use the term geology to describe that science.

MARIA THERESA (1717–1780) Queen of Austria-Hungary, a practical-minded ruler who put into effect many social, religious and educational reforms.

ANTONIO VALLISNERI (The Younger) (1708–1777) Professor of natural history at the University of Padua. Like his famous scientist father, he doubted the theory of spontaneous generation, and encouraged Spallanzani to investigate the problem.

SELECTED BIBLIOGRAPHY

Adams, A. E. "Lazzaro Spallanzani (1729–1799)." *Scientific Monthly*, Vol. 29 (1929), pp. 529–37.

Bulloch, W. "Spontaneous Generation and Heterogenesis," *The History of Bacteriology*. London: Oxford University Press, 1938.

Burget, G. E. "Lazzaro Spallanzani (1729–1799)." *Annals of Medical History*, Vol. 6 (1924), pp. 177–84.

Franchini, G. "Lazzaro Spallanzani (1729–1799)." *Annals of Medical History*, n.s. Vol. 2 (1930), pp. 56–62.

Gasking, Elizabeth B. "New Discoveries and New Attitudes, 1680–1745," *Rise of Experimental Biology*. New York: Random House, 1970.

Hamilton, J. B. "The Shadowed Side of Spallanzani." *Yale Journal of Biology and Medicine*, Vol. 7 (1934–35), pp. 151–70.

Prescott, F. "Spallanzani on Spontaneous Generation and Digestion." *Proceedings of the Royal Society of Medicine*, Vol. 23 (1930), pp. 495–510.

SAM and BERYL EPSTEIN have written more than fifty books. The titles range over a wide variety of subjects. They have written two previous books for Coward, McCann & Geoghegan's Science Discovery Series—*Mister Peale's Mammoth*, which was a Junior Literary Guild selection, and *Dr. Beaumont and the Man With the Hole in His Stomach*.

The Epsteins live in Southold, New York.

JANE STERRETT is a graduate of the Rhode Island School of Design and received an M.F.A. from Yale University. She has been represented in many group shows and exhibits. Ms. Sterrett illustrated Thomas Mann's *Death in Venice and Other Stories* in the Franklin Library limited edition. In addition to doing freelance illustration and design, she is presently on the faculties of Pratt Institute and Parsons School of Design.